1977 BENJAMIN F. FAIRLESS MEMORIAL LECTURES

Library of Congress Catalog Card Number 78-58383

ISBN Number 0-915604-16-7

The Multinational Corporation
Its Manners, Methods and Myths

Monroe E. Spaght

Carnegie-Mellon University Press

Distributed by Columbia University Press
New York — Guilford, Surrey

The Benjamin F. Fairless Memorial Lectures endowment fund has been established at Carnegie-Mellon University to support an annual series of lectures. An internationally known figure from the world of business, government, or education is invited each year to present three lectures at Carnegie-Mellon under the auspices of its Graduate School of Industrial Administration. In general, the lectures will be concerned with some aspects of business or public administration; the relationships between business and government, management and labor; or a subject related to the themes of preserving economic freedom, human liberty, and the strengthening of individual enterprise — all of which were matters of deep concern to Mr. Fairless throughout his career.

Mr. Fairless was president of United States Steel Corporation for fifteen years, and chairman of the board from 1952 until his retirement in 1955. A friend of Carnegie-Mellon University for many years, he served on the board of trustees from 1952 until his death. In 1959 he was named honorary chairman of the board.

Mr. Fairless died January 1, 1962.

Monroe E. Spaght was born near Eureka, California, in 1909. He studied chemistry and physics at Stanford University and the University of Leipzig, and received his Ph.D. in Chemistry from Stanford in 1933. In that same year he joined Shell as a research chemist.

In 1949 he became president of Shell Development Company, Shell's research affiliate, and later served as Executive Vice President, and then President, of Shell Oil Company.

Mr. Spaght was appointed a Managing Director of the Royal Dutch/Shell Group of Companies and Chairman of Shell Oil Company in 1965. He retired in 1970 from these positions, but continues to be a director of the Royal Dutch Petroleum Company, several Shell companies, and several other companies both in the United States and in Europe.

Mr. Spaght has long been an active spokesman for business in scientific and educational fields. He is a former trustee of Stanford University and director of the Stanford Research Institute. At Shell, he was founder and long-time president of the Shell Companies Foundation, Inc. which pioneered several programs in support of education. Mr. Spaght served on advisory committees for Princeton and Harvard, was chairman of the Committee for Corporate Support of American Universities, and has received seven honorary degrees as well as awards, decorations, and citations both in the U.S. and abroad. He is a member of the National Academy of Engineering, a fellow of the American Association for the Advancement of Science, and a past president of the Society of Chemical Industry.

In his introduction to one of Mr. Spaght's books, *The Bright Key,* former HEW Secretary and Common Cause chairman John Gardner wrote: "The reader will find . . . a vigorous, open pragmatic mind at work, a mind by nature calm and reflective, by training penetrating and rational, at home with science and technology, but equally at home with questions of human performance. The modern world needs men who can work with complex organizations yet retain their individuality, who can master technology yet retain their humanity, who can move easily between reflection and action. This book is written by such a man."

1977

The Multinational Corporation
Its Manners, Methods and Myths

nine

Introduction

I am honored indeed to be invited to give the 1977 Fairless Memorial Lectures, particularly so when I see the list of distinguished people who have preceded me. I have had the pleasure of knowing several of them.

In this connection it was my special privilege to have known Mr. Fairless also. In New York City, during the early 1950s, I was a new initiate of a businessman's club of which he was a senior and respected member. He befriended me as would an uncle, and his repeated kindnesses were too many to mention. Of all my recollections, however, the most memorable was an occasion when Mr. Fairless was being introduced to an audience of outsiders who were the guests of our club. Mr. Cason Calloway, of Atlanta, Georgia — a director of U.S. Steel at the time — was making the introduction. He knew Mr. Fairless very well, was saying a number of highly complimentary things about him, and among them — and this I shall never forget — he said "I really think that Ben Fairless wouldn't know how to tell a lie!" What an accolade! He was held in the highest regard and with the greatest affection by all whose lives he touched. I am honored to have my name associated with his memory.

It was at that very time to which I refer, in 1953 to be exact, that I had just said good-bye to my beloved world of science and research, and, with a final renunciation of vows, entered the world of business: indeed, international business. Twenty years before, 1933, just back from study in Germany, and the proud possessor of a brand new Ph.D. degree in Chemistry, I was a young instructor in the Department of Chemistry at Stanford University in California. The Shell Oil people wanted a few young scientists for their new research programs in California and they came by Stanford. My professors advised me to accept the offer they made me. "You might even like it!", one of them said. Well — apparently I did, or at least I have spent nearly 45 years giving it a trial!

The years that followed 1933 were eventful. After some years of research and then technical assignments with Shell Oil in California, World War II came, and I had a myriad of industry-government assignments, and then service in Europe and later Japan on technical missions. After the war, and for the following years until 1953, I was again deeply engrossed in Shell research. First — our Dutch colleagues had been under military occupation for years, and our British colleagues had had their research programs quite severely fragmented. They needed the help of their American colleagues, whose science and technology had burgeoned through the war. And — in putting it all back together — Shell Oil and the research companies of the Royal Dutch-Shell Group developed a coordinated and cost-sharing program designed to yield each side the most research results per dollar. I had the privilege of a leading part in putting this all together and then of heading up the Shell Oil research company for several years.

The Royal Dutch-Shell Group has been strongly science-oriented from the beginning and has always given great attention to its research and technology. They have always reasoned that in this world, where "ownership" or "possession" of anything can be quite transient, one's brain, one's knowledge, is the one, last impregnable citadel. The overall worldwide research program to which I refer is one of the broadest and largest industrial research projects in existence. This year that total program will cost over $250 million.

I have told you all this only to say that you are being addressed by a person who is, at heart, a physical scientist. If such a person is true to his discipline, he lives largely in a world of facts and numbers. He is trained to respect the truth, and particularly to expect that his propositions will be examined and judged by fact, not by prejudice or wish. He also tends to be impatient with allegations that aren't subjected to similar analysis and proof.

In these three lectures I want to talk about some things I have seen in these nearly 25 years of my post-research and science career, but seen still through the eyes of that particular breed, the physical scientist. Of course, three lectures — or indeed thirty — wouldn't suffice to record everything that one recalls from an eventful career. Therefore, I have had to choose a few subjects from the many, and I know that they may not always be the ones about which you would want most to hear. I do hope, however, that you will not find them uninteresting.

In Chapter 1, under the title of "Manners," I talk about a very large multinational enterprise. By "manners" I don't mean good or bad, but rather the Webster definition that "manners" is a way of acting, habits, customs, nature. As I have said, my comments will concern aspects of my own choosing, but I hope that they will interest you and that they might even give some of you some useful thoughts.

In Chapter 2, under the heading of "Methods," I discuss some of our procedures, particularly about making the major decisions that are so determining.

Under the third title, "Myths," I talk about some other aspects of a world-wide enterprise, particularly about how it is seen and judged by some, and about areas where facts seem to have little respect and where a scientist finds his classical weapons of limited use.

* * *

As I am addressing an American audience, perhaps I had better declare the fact that I have had, and still have, two separate and distinct Shell hats and tell you which I am wearing. I am a Director of Shell Oil Company in Houston, and that in itself is the thirteenth largest company in the U.S.A. in terms of 1976 sales, increasingly a multinational enterprise in its own operations. But as a Director of Royal Dutch Petroleum Company I also have a Group parent company hat, which is the one I am wearing for these lectures.

Some of what I have to say relates to the Group outside the U.S.A. and not to Shell Oil Company here. If that sounds rather involved, it is, but the Shell Group is, I believe, exceptional in having such a large publicly quoted company within a larger publicly quoted company. We recognize the proper distinction between the two — even if one is, in terms of ultimate financial results, a large part of the other.

I should add that my remarks concerning Group practices, procedures and policies should be understood in the following context: in every case the laws of the country where an operating company is operating are observed, and nothing is done which impinges upon the independence and autonomy of the company under that country's laws or which would be harmful to minority stockholders.

The Multinational Corporation
Its Manners, Methods
and Myths

I. Manners

I. MANNERS

We of the Royal Dutch-Shell Group often claim that we are the most multinational — or transnational — of any business venture anywhere. The claim isn't always accepted without protest, because there are Unilevers and Nestlés in the world, to say nothing of Eastman Kodaks and General Motors and Exxons, and so on. But, without arguing the point, there are about 270 Shell operating companies in over 100 countries around the world. They involve total gross assets of about 35 billion dollars; they handle each day over 5 million barrels of oil (about 1/10 of the world's total), and 7 billion cubic feet of gas. Total Shell chemical companies' operations add up to one of the world's very largest chemical enterprises. We are also engaged in coal, metals, and nuclear energy. We had gross sales last year of 42 billion dollars, and net income of 2¼ billion dollars — 5% on sales.

Some companies are multinational by evolving from a single domestic base, but some are multinational by parentage, and Royal Dutch-Shell is an outstanding example. You may be interested in a brief resume of how it all came about.

Towards the end of the last century, a small company called the Royal Dutch Petroleum Co. had discovered oil in what was then known as the Dutch East Indies (now Indonesia). It developed its discoveries, built refineries, and began to market products, particularly kerosene, in the Far East. The main business was, literally, "oil for the lamps of China." Its money and talents were consumed in production and refining, while its rapidly growing volumes needed transportation and marketing expansion. Also, in the market place it was encountering both American and Russian competition. It could use help.

Quite independent of all this, there was a London-based firm, known as The "Shell" Transport and Trading Company. Its name had come some years before when its then head, one of the famed Samuel family of London, had taken his daughter on a summer trip on one of their ships to the Far

East. The girl picked up a pecten shell on one of the beaches, took it home and made an ornament of it for her bedroom dresser. The father had some more shells brought back as items to sell, and soon such shells were prominently found in the homes of Victorian England. The company was subsequently named The "Shell" Transport and Trading Company. By then, however, Samuel had already begun, as part of his transport and trading activities, the movement of Russian kerosene from the Caspian to the Far East, and the sale of it through outlets that he had established there. Oil became an ever larger and more important part of his total business. However, Samuel lacked security of supply under his Russian contracts, and he had begun to move ever increasing quantities from Royal Dutch.

Royal Dutch and Shell saw themselves as complementary, and they sensed that unless they made some sort of arrangement, they could just both fall victim to Rockefeller's Standard Oil.

There ensued, in 1907, just 70 years ago, the merging of their combined assets into the Royal Dutch-Shell Group, with Royal Dutch owning 60% and "Shell" Transport and Trading 40% of the total. The ownership continues today exactly as then. Nearly everything around the world that bears the name Shell — the trade name and emblem that the Group adopted upon its formation in 1907 — is owned upstream 60/40 by those two parent companies. The same is true of our share of ownership in many joint ventures with other companies, or groups of companies, around the world. There are two particular exceptions. Here in the United States, 30% of the shares of Shell Oil Company are in the hands of the public, with 70% owned upstream by the parents, in the ratio 60/40. Likewise, in Canada, 21% of the shares of Shell Canada are owned by the public, and 79% upstream by the parents.

We are indeed multinational. There are five nationalities (Dutch, British, American, French and German) represented on the boards of the two parent companies. There are four (Dutch, British, American and French) in the ranks of the

Committee of Managing Directors, the body of eight (at this time) who are the senior executives at holding company level, and at least 25 nationalities are in very senior positions in the operating companies around the world. Our employees, although only slightly over 150,000 in number, represent more than 100 different nationalities.

Shares of either Royal Dutch or "Shell" Transport and Trading are quoted on stock exchanges in Austria, Belgium, France, Luxembourg, the Netherlands, Switzerland, the United Kingdom, the United States and West Germany. We have in total over a million shareholders. Of the two parent companies, the United Kingdom shareholding is the largest, nearly 40%, the Netherlands next at 24%, the United States and Switzerland each at about 13%, France at 7%, and essentially all the rest in Germany, Belgium and Luxembourg.

The Group has principal service companies in London and The Hague which, as far as practicable, operate as though they were one, although modern developments in legislation for worker participation in management may increasingly separate them. They employ people of 20 different nationalities, and represent a storehouse of experience and expertise perhaps unique in the oil industry.

It is not surprising that from the alliance back in 1907 each of the parents' central office locations retains some of its original identity. Thus, the more "science" type functions (Research, Exploration and Production, Manufacturing etc.) are centered in The Hague, and the more "business" type functions (Marketing, Finance, Supplies, Shipping etc.) are centered in London.

Perhaps that is enough for background information. Let us then go to work and talk first about how so vast an organization is kept on course.

Actually, it's not all that difficult!

First of all, there is one "Group" language, English. Of course, many of our people are linguists of the first order. As one of my Dutch colleagues put it: "In Holland, a good 8-iron shot in any direction puts you in the land of another language! Hence, we must learn languages." Indeed they do!

Discard language as a barrier.

Methods and mores vary. In the Islamic countries there is Ramadan, but also there is Lent in Christian countries, Independence Day in the United States, and the Queen's Birthday in Holland and the U.K. These are not barriers.

At this moment about 3,300 expatriates of more than 50 different nationalities work for Shell companies in countries other than their own. This cadre of international staff is most important in maintaining technical, business, social and legal standards Group-wide. It makes for coherence of approach.

Candidates for key jobs learn to speak a common language, to attain an understanding of the international dimension by their experience in countries other than their own, and to share in common training experiences.

In total, what I am wanting to say is that the Group make-up of many nationalities spread over the entire earth is no problem in today's world of easy communication and transportation. Indeed, I have come to believe that it is the reverse. One comes to know, to expect, and to welcome the fact that around the table are going to be some who might see the problem differently. One comes to appreciate that his own views are not sacrosanct, that there are other factors to weigh, that what makes sense in California could be totally unacceptable in a land not all that far away!

Well — you say — tell us more about how you operate! Let me begin by saying that through the years I have seen several different systems and philosophies used. Some have clearly been better than others, but I have come to one basic conclusion. It is that there is no one best and right form of management structure. What is best at one time or for one group of people will not necessarily be the best at another time or for another group of people, or possible under governmental constraints.

I confess to some impatience with writers who propound one scheme of organization as the one and only, or who talk about delegation of authority, for example, as though it were a new concept. Similarly, there is the tiresome character who has convinced himself, for example, that an executive should have exactly seven people answer to him, not six and not eight.

As I say, there are many "right" forms of organization. My view is simply that one should be flexible and fit the design to the people and the situation involved.

A general system that appeals to me, after having seen the many different ones we have tried, is basically the one now used and it operates as follows. I am referring, of course, to wholly-owned companies: different systems may apply where there is outside equity.

Central to the co-ordination of the Royal Dutch-Shell Group is a Committee of Managing Directors (the C.M.D.) appointed to consider, develop and decide overall objectives and long term plans to be recommended to the wholly-owned operating companies concerned with day to day Shell businesses around the world. We call them Group Managing Directors because we cannot think of a more accurate title that is tolerably short. However, they do not operationally manage the Group as such; how could they? They are appointed by the two Parent Companies to manage, in effect, the shareholder role. The most obvious shareholder role in a large Group is the overall financial look which is ultimately reflected in the Group accounts.

Other roles involve personnel planning for top jobs — to which I shall revert later — objectives and long term planning for the wholly-owned subsidiaries. You could say that the C.M.D. is not concerned to manage the Operating Companies around the world so much as the glue that holds them together; and that covers the co-ordination of at least a part of our principal resources which are people, oil and gas, and money.

This Committee has varied in number in recent decades from five to eight. It is currently eight, of whom five are from the Royal Dutch side and three from "Shell" Transport and Trading. As I said earlier, four nationalities (Dutch, British, American and French) are represented and the individuals combine a wide range of disciplines — economics, science, engineering, law, finance and the humanities. Most of them have headed up one or more large Shell companies somewhere around the world.

Each Managing Director has spheres of interest which are partly functional and partly regional. That is to say, one M.D. may be concerned with Exploration and Production activities and at the same time with Shell companies' operations in Africa; another, say, with Marketing and with the work of the companies in the Far East. This does not mean that he is trying to "manage" by remote control the operations of any given Shell company, or companies, on the other side of the world. Each company has its own Chief Executive who is responsible to its own board. But the Managing Director concerned will be in close contact with the Chief Executive of each company within his sphere of interest and be in a position to assess its results. Naturally, shareholders can change a company's management if things go so awry that this is judged necessary, but fortunately that is a very little used power of ultimate resort.

I hope that all this does not sound too aloof and impersonal. In fact, the heads of operating companies are men of high caliber, in some cases running enterprises which are large by any standards; their counterparts in the service companies in London and The Hague are men of proved ability who have in their time borne similar responsibilities in the field. They know each other well, and they share a common code of values developed over many years.

Now a word about the functional responsibilities of Managing Directors. The functional M.D. of Exploration and Production, for example, is responsible for maintaining the strength and excellence of this central office organization. It is not the responsibility of this M.D., or his central office organization, to see that their talents are used everywhere in operation. That tends to be on the shoulders of the operating company head, and his failure to seek all possible help and expertise from them is his shortcoming.

Thus, each part of the world receives individual attention from an M.D., and each M.D. at the same time maintains a global view through the eyes of one or more central office functions.

Because of the world-wide nature of the operations involved, certain activities such as Oil Supplies and Marine Transportation are necessarily central functions — not without input from the field, and not without their co-operation and general agreement, of course. Perhaps I should repeat that throughout my general remarks I am not talking about companies such as Shell Oil and Shell Canada, which are independently managed, but the wholly-owned Group companies. Clearly the supply of crude oil to upward of 50 refineries in more than 30 countries around the world, with all the marine scheduling involved, must be organized and executed largely at the center. Likewise, Finance and Personnel, for example, have activities at the center that can concern operating companies all over the world.

Obviously, with M.Ds. whose backgrounds include experience in some of the functions and most of whom have had experience as well as heads of operating companies, there is constant interplay between the different groups, and any failure by Deutsche Shell, for example, to seek help from the central Manufacturing function on a major project would reflect poorly on all parties concerned.

Here, then, is one way to co-ordinate a multinational enterprise with parents of different nationalities and with a wide scope of interests. In Chapter 2 I will talk about some of our experiences through the years, particularly about some of the major decisions that have been so important to our success — and our failure. But while on the matter of organization, there is one matter of decision-making that is concerned with it, and therefore let me deal with it now.

One gives his eligible young people every opportunity to develop, to be trained. They are given a variety of assignments and experiences. All of this is fairly straight forward. However, then comes repeatedly the need to make selection for advancement, and, when it is concerned with the more senior and then the very top jobs, it is a matter of the greatest importance to the whole enterprise.

I want to speak on this matter most seriously, because it is of such paramount importance. It is important, of course, to have good people at all levels. The great scientist or engineer can do much for a company, as did C.E.K. Mees for Eastman Kodak, Irving Langmuir for General Electric, Doc Kettering for General Motors or Wallace Carothers for du Pont. Although, clearly, the good manager at any level is valuable, outstanding corporate performance is almost always related to the top executives — indeed, the top executive; and the cause of poor or catastrophic performance almost always has to do with the incompetence at the top.

Occasionally it is fraudulence, but most commonly it is incompetence. There was a famous motion-picture company in Hollywood that was reduced to nothing by a chief executive who neither looked after it nor allowed anyone else to do so.

There was the case of a company, again in the U.S., that went from a fine position practically to bankruptcy while its chief executive sat on the boards of 13 outside companies.

I know a former chief executive, who left successively two companies on the verge of collapse, who, in the midst of it, maintained that in order for a chief executive to have a broad perspective, he should have several active outside business interests in addition to the company he runs.

But these are examples of revealed incompetence. Unfortunately, much more common are the companies that limp along, performing at half potential, because they are not properly managed. In contrast, the record is replete with examples of a mediocre, lackadaisical company that somehow gets a good leader and is transformed in a few years into one of the best.

The common culprit in all these stories, good and bad, is, of course, top management.

Let me end my chronicle of all the things that can go wrong — or right — and get back to the matter of how it all happens. Training people and selecting those for promotion is part of the lives of all of us in any organization, large or small. To all of you who have had roles in this area, I wouldn't be surprised if mentioning the subject brings some sad memories to mind. I know that it does to me!

I want to make the assumption that good people are always available. You may say that is rather a brave assumption, because, unfortunately, sometimes an obviously qualified person just does not seem to be around. But that is in itself a condemnation of the system, because good young people are always available.

The crime of poor selection for promotion, of poor choices at the lower levels, leads to the ultimate tragedy of incompetence at the very top. The selecting of people for promotion is perhaps the most unscientific, ephemeral and dangerous bit of decision-making that anyone faces in his corporate life. As I said, it is an activity in which we all take part, because it involves everyone in the company from the lowest levels of management. Ironically, the ultimate and most vital decisions, the selection of the top people, commonly involve directors, some of whom are the least able to exercise good judgment, not because of lack of ability but because of their limited exposure to the individuals involved.

I suggest that the reasons why we sometimes do so poorly in people-decision are many.

One of them is that we are guessing what an individual will do in circumstances in which we have never seen him perform. We may have seen him in similar circumstances, but not quite the same. The qualities of leadership are hard to define, and it is never possible to predict with assurance how anyone will respond to the very particular environment in which he will be found.

I think often of the remark of a friend of mine back in 1952, when Harry S. Truman was retiring from the presidency after about seven years in office. You may remember that the Republican candidate was General Eisenhower and the Democratic candidate was Mr. Adlai Stevenson. My friend said that there was only one man about whom we could have a firm opinion as to what sort of president he would make, and that was Harry S. Truman. Neither of the others had ever been seen in the job.

Another reason for our troubles in selecting the right person is that here is one of the few areas of decision-making where human emotion is prominently involved. Years ago, in California, I was a young technologist in one of our large refineries, and periodically there was an evaluation of all of us by the non-technical people who managed the refinery. I recall so vividly that, again and again, some one of us would be described as a very good or very able technologist, and hence one who was eligible for promotion.

The fact of being termed by them "a good technologist" meant usually that he was an affable character, that they liked him, that he got along well. And as for being eligible for promotion, I have never been able to see that this follows logically from being good at what one is doing.

A persistent pit-fall is this matter of promoting a man because he is doing his present job well. In a process industry, like Shell, the good geologist or technologist or engineer is valuable, and his good works are seen. The ambitious people always want more authority, a bigger say, a larger salary, a title, and one cannot expect them to say no to a promotion that almost always involves more management.

But the combination of pressure from the bottom and emotional response from the top results in some of the oddest things in a large corporation.

Good engineers are ruined because they are not good managers. An outstanding young scientist gets an award of some sort, and the limelight shines briefly on him. He has demonstrated unusual ability in a particular field, and there ensues a clamor on all sides, up, down and sideways, for him to be promoted into management.

But the crime of advancing the wrong person because he or she is outstanding in something that may have little to do with management-talents is probably less than the equally common one of advancing the one who happens to be next in line. A vacancy occurs, for any reason, and the local assistant or a parallel assistant with longer service is given the job. It is the easiest and the most decent thing to do and it will probably work out. He might surprise us all. Indeed, possibly he will, but probably he will not. It can work out in the worst possible way: it will not be so bad that he has to be removed, it will be just good enough to make removal awkward and just bad enough to ensure that the organization carries on in a mediocre way.

This is a common pattern and in my opinion perhaps the most common one that results in the average organization. As I said before, the good people are usually there, but it is an inexcusable lack of analysis and courage that so commonly leads to the promotion of the wrong or, at best, the average one.

No doubt I speak as though picking the 'right' person is easy, if we only have the courage and a little bit of common sense. If it were only that easy! What qualities do we look for in the outstanding executive? Basically, it is the extreme difficulty in answering that question that causes so many tragedies in this area of decision-making. A thousand writers have put down their own lists of qualities of this hypothetical outstanding executive. You know them all as well as I do. But while we all agree that this person should be honest and sincere, and twenty other things, his or her success as an executive seems to depend on some qualities that are hard to define in words. How that person influences an organization involves qualities of behavior that are very hard to describe, let alone quantify.

And, of course, another complicating factor is that one person may be right for one time but wrong for another. We can dream of the "man for all seasons," and perhaps he does sometimes exist. However, the one needed for a time of ebullient expansion may not be the one if the company must be rescued from the brink of bankruptcy.

All right, you say, now that he's got all that out of his system, what is he or they trying to do about it?

Well, actually, we are trying and in a fashion that pleases a scientist. There are people, professional psychologists and that sort, who believe there are particular observable qualities in a person, not especially noticed in normal circumstances nor ever subjected to measurement, that do portend unusual executive ability. These qualities, they believe, can be measured as one would measure an ability with languages, for example. We now employ and retain such people and try to understand everything they have in mind.

I don't know how successful we will be in these new efforts, but I sincerely believe that all of us can improve our performance in this area of executive preparation and, particularly, selection.

In the following chapter, I want to discuss a broad range of subjects for decision-making, where the choices have been and will be of great importance to the corporate venture. We will see again that some of them are subject to beautiful, clear-cut analyses, but others will see the scientist adrift from his world of fact and reliability. I hope that the examples will interest you, and some will even amuse you. To those involved, however, I assure you that some of them were anything but amusing!

The Multinational Corporation
Its Manners, Methods
and Myths

II. Methods

II. METHODS

A few years ago, on a London-New York flight, a young man sitting next to me asked me to explain to him what an 'executive' does. He said that, in my business, he could understand what a truck driver does, what a service station attendant does, even what the manager of an oil refinery does, but what does a Managing Director or a Chief Executive do?

Of course, he does many things — some of them mundane, unchallenging, not uncommonly difficult. But, most importantly, it seems to me, and of greatest demand and difficulty, he makes or participates in the making of the major decisions that direct his enterprise.

These decisions can be the answers to relatively simple questions. Shall we increase the dividend? They can concern more complicated matters. Shall we now attempt a major invasion of a certain new field of business activity and, if so, how? But, whatever the question, they are of particular importance to the enterprises we manage.

Here is where the senior executive of the large company lives. What he does, to answer my young friend, is a task that sounds very prosaic, very unglamorous, and very lifeless: he makes major decisions.

In the world of movies and television, the executive in big business is indeed a glamorous character. He's a high-powered operator — telephones ringing, secretaries rushing about. He spouts forth clear-cut, staccato decisions that come from his superb intellect and complete knowledge of the subject. If such a person exists, I have neither seen him nor heard of him. An important decision is often reached haltingly after the most colorless, dull and heart-searching effort. And, when the decision is made, it is probably with some measure of uncertainty and lingering worry about the choice that has been made. In those agonizing hours, no one could appreciate help more than the individual who sits in lonely isolation and has no further court of appeal. Any new technique or method of forecast would have a warm welcome indeed.

For those of us whose lives have been more or less a series of these hours, we come to wonder about how much better management methods might become and whether one day we can approach the motion picture version of rapidfire decision-making as a result of having at our command complete information and data such that all errors of judgment will have been taken out of the process.

I have wondered often just what the future might bring in this area to help us do better. You can imagine, then, my interest when some time ago I received a copy of a news release from a prominent American research institute announcing a series of seminars in the U.S. on the subject of decision analysis, a new discipline to help organizations make strategic decisions. It stated that "an increasing number of large corporations as well as government agencies are relying on decision analysis to help solve their problems." It explained that "decision analysis provides a logical framework to put all factors that influence a decision — no matter how uncertain — into explicit economic terms."

I confess that over the years I have developed a resistance, even an immunity, to new claptrap of this or any sort; my developed impulse is to swear and cast aside any such new language. That immunity has come about through years of struggling to find my way through automation, operations research, the frightful new jargon about models, programming and computers, and now the necessity, I am told, of having differing strategies with varying scenarios to face a decision as complicated as what airline and flight to take from London to New York.

As a long-time research scientist it isn't any resistance on my part to welcome something new — quite the contrary — but it has been a tiresome quest to find anything other than old common sense in such new jargon as operations research, etc.

So now here comes yet another new one, and this one will enable us to put all factors that influence a decision — no matter how uncertain — into explicit economic terms!

I want to be among the first to compliment those individuals and organizations that have been making fine contributions to infusing better methods of analysis into certain kinds of business problems. Unfortunately, one tends to get the impression that new methods of decision-making will open a new day for the executive where all his decisions will be clean, crisp, clear, and right. I do not think that day is about to come, and I see much of the executive's decision-making of the future still laborious, painful, and painfully inexact. This is why this recent announcement brought a certain feeling of sadness to me.

I want to talk in this chapter about why I feel this way. In doing so, my observations will be personal, but they will probably be consonant with the opinions of my colleagues in Shell companies. While they will concern our particular ventures, they will apply to other companies and countries, for the problems in this area seem to me to be much the same everywhere.

While corporate decisions include everything from the trivial to the impossible, to be practical let's leave out the trivia of daily housekeeping and think about those facts of choosing among alternatives on subjects where the decision is of major importance to our business.

I haven't been able ever to divide the spectrum of these important acts of deciding into neat boxes or divisions. Each one of you could produce his own classification. One could, for example, rate decision-making problems according to the reliability, or rigidity, or fidelity of the assumptions going into the consideration. Are they fact or judgment or pure chance?

I would like to try something like that by discussing a few differing areas of decision-making. They will not attempt to encompass all of the decisions in your day or mine, but hopefully they will illustrate the kinds of variables that go into the equations. At the same time, we might try to see what likelihood there is that new methods and machines will help solve these problems that fill the business executive's day.

Let met talk first about the area that the people who

announced those seminars have, or should have, particularly in mind. The methods they are teaching are not new. One might say that the science is not new, but possibly the operating technology is. Their methods formalize into equations and relationships the data that are known and then give them reasonably rigid mathematical treatment. You will then see in numbers and graphs the relationships which before you may have felt but not known finitely; indeed, the analyses may reveal relationships that you did not sense before.

For example, if you have a multi-variable manufacturing system — that is, let us say, several factories, several products from each factory, several different patterns of transportation of raw materials and products — such analyses can do much to tell you how to operate most efficiently, whether you may be making some products in the wrong place, perhaps whether you should enlarge one factory and shut another down, etc.

Into these equations one may put also estimates of future demands for his different products, with varying growth estimates for different ones and in different areas. One can estimate the strength of the competition, indeed, many other variables as well, and there will come out a preferred program — now, in sophisticated language, called a strategy, or a scenario of a particular strategy, etc.

Such decision-making analyses can indeed be used in studying a possible acquisition, let us say.

We will estimate the effect of this acquisition on our ability to compete, or on relevant market factors, on operating costs, reduction of the research bill, central office cost reduction, etc. and, against the case of not making the acquisition, learn what we should be prepared to pay for the acquisition, and so forth.

In Western Europe there are 20 Shell refineries of varying capacities and complexities. They operate on a diet of more than 30 different crude oils, supplying over 2,500 different products at the rate of nearly 100 million gallons per day through a most complicated distribution system, serving a population of over 300 million people. A European operating model tells us exactly how to coordinate this multivariable system in order to optimize efficiency. Indeed, it will tell us what crude oils to feed to each refinery. It will give in any desired detail the operating conditions within each refinery, down to the reactor temperature of an individual reforming or cracking unit. It will prescribe the exact product flows through pipelines, ships and trucks. We are told exactly how to operate every piece of this great complicated system.

Now to me, as a scientist, I completely embrace and applaud the work of all who make available to the world of business increased awareness and knowledge of these types of information analysis in order to allow more informed decision-making. I have been in organizations that try to make the greatest use of such analyses, and I attest to the fact that they are most helpful.

With the help of computers, these techniques are at the least great time savers, and at the most they show us things that we might otherwise not have seen.

They are most applicable in systems where there are perhaps many variables, but where the variables are subject to being assigned good, reliable values. It is great fun to design, with the help of computers, the most intricate chemical plant or the most complicated distribution or transportation systems, because here we tend to deal with firm numbers and relationships.

But it would be unfair to these people if I implied that the methods they teach in their seminars are applicable solely to situations where the variables can be reliably and rigorously evaluated. Instead, they teach a broader philosophy.

They teach us to examine critically what we think we know, to try to put numbers or number relationships to our opinions, to assume varying situations that are out of our control, and, then, from a rigid machine treatment of all this, to come to understand better what can happen, how critical are the different assumptions; these enable, finally, the choice of one path, having now greater knowledge of what the country may look like as we go down the path, and what to do when the scenery changes in a certain way.

But, as I said, whenever I read the announcement of another decision-making seminar, my deepest feeling is one of melancholy, of sadness, sort of a feeling of despair.

Why does that come to me?

It is basically because, in my life in business, a majority of the most important decisions, those that really matter, seem to be made with systems of variables that are not firm or reliably known. Here, then, is my second type or class of decisions. This type involves assumptions or guesses of situations over which we have little control, or it relies on judgments where there are no numbers or equations to help.

There are so many areas of business decision-making where methods and machines offer little hope. Political events are just about impossible to anticipate. A political or economic crisis can originate in a fashion that no human being can possibly predict. It can follow from some act of God, a human death, an accident utterly beyond prediction.

Here is an area of human judgment where knowledge, feel, educated hunch and sensible courage can be of value completely beyond that of the machine-derived decision as to how large any new installation should be or whether the acquisition is worth ten million dollars more or less.

We have been talking about decisions that are in the direct interests of a company. But equally well there fit in here matters such as those involving social objectives. Here lie responsibilities, and opportunities, that need the most thoughtful evaluation and action. It seems clear that from here on our multinational corporations will be central features in society's mechanism for regulating its environment. Industry will supply much of the information — facts, data, research, experience, etc. — on which the plans of society will be based. In many instances, industry must and does lead, and there will be a never-ending need for it to participate with intelligent and constructive attitudes and actions. This calls for a class of decisions where machines and methods probably can't help, but where the best of judgment will be demanded.

Then, there is a morality in business that is more commonly manifested than that for which we are credited. I have a good illustration.

Some years ago a very good friend of mine, Jack Daley, was then the head of one of the main operating divisions of the du Pont Company. He told me about an experience of his which I have often found worth repeating. At that time, when a du Pont operating division head needed approval for a major capital project he took it to the so-called Executive Committee, which was composed of the chairman of the company, the president, and several vice-presidents such as the head of research, etc. On this occasion the chairman was the legendary Mr. Walter Carpenter, for years the most distinguished head of du Pont.

Jack was bringing a proposal to the Executive Committee which involved the construction by du Pont of a new plant manufacturing one product, a chemical intermediate, all of which was to be sold to one customer who was going to build a plant alongside that of du Pont. Jack made his presentation to the committee, and at the end of it, as he sat down, he thought to himself he had made such a complete presentation and it was such a sound project that he did not see how even a question could be asked. Mr. Carpenter asked his colleagues if they had any questions; a few routine ones followed and finally Mr. Carpenter said, "Very well, Jack, I have only one question and it is this, are you sure that the deal is fair to your customer?" Daley said that it was the last question that ever would have arisen in his mind — the customer could be expected to look out for himself — and he was so taken aback that he could not even reply. Mr. Carpenter said, "I won't ask you to answer it now, but when you can answer that in the affirmative to yourself, then you have our approval to proceed." Daley said that that experience had a profound effect on him through his whole career.

No machine or decision-making method was involved. Here was only the feeling and judgment of a moral, sensitive human being.

The issues raised here, be they Walter Carpenter's questions or the prior matters of social responsibility, are going to be more and not less demanding of the executive's judgment from here on.

Self-service will not be enough, yet careless crusading can be disastrous.

But let me turn back specifically to the multinational group I know best, where size and complexity compound the uncertainties of decision-making.

Among the most risky decisions that have to be taken by any group of oil companies has to do with where to look for its basic resource. Only about one well in nine discovers oil; only about one in 30 leads to the development of a commercial oil or gas field. Moreover, the lead time between discovery and production is inevitably long, and the political hazards are enormous.

I should like to give you two or three examples of decision-making in this hazardous area, both inside and outside the United States, some of which have turned out well and some badly.

Notably here at home, Shell Oil let the East Texas field slip through its fingers. More than half a century ago the Roxana Petroleum Corp. (one of the predecessors of Shell Oil) did some exploring in East Texas but with little success. Then two young prospectors offered us what we call a farm-out. If we would drill one well, one wildcat, we would earn 50% of whatever was developed. These young men had a firm hunch about where that one well should be drilled — they just had a feeling, they said. But we, not to be influenced by such unscientific silliness, made the best geological analysis we could, and it contradicted that of our two young friends. Eventually we drilled a well where the experts recommended and it was a dry hole. We pulled out.

Ten years later, on October 3, 1939, a penniless 70 year old wildcatter happily named Columbus Joiner (or, as history records him — Dad Joiner) drilled at about the exact spot that the two young prospectors urged us to choose, and he discovered the largest oilfield then or since found in the United States. From that time onwards the history of the East Texas Field was written in superlatives. Had Shell made the discovery, it has been suggested that we would easily have become — and soon — the largest oil company in the U.S.

In the early 1960s, some state lease sales were announced for the far north of Alaska. I shall never forget the day that we in Shell Oil had to decide whether to bid for some of those leases. Our people were most unenthusiastic. It was in an extremely remote area. No one knew much about the subsurface geology of the region. More important, we had good land holdings farther inland, to the south, in Alaska, and the prospects for oil there were equally good. Further, we were quite completely employed elsewhere looking for oil.

We decided not to participate. I take responsibility for the final decision. In the areas involved in these sales there has now been proved something approaching 10 billion barrels of oil. Three or four of our competitors will do well financially with those properties; despite the fact that the Alyeska pipeline has in fact cost well over ten times the original estimate, and obstructions by the environmentalists, etc. delayed construction for at least four years. But, fortunately for our successful competitors, the value of oil on the West Coast is now about $14 per barrel instead of the $2 prevailing 15 years ago.

I have mentioned a couple of cases where, as Shakespeare says, we in Shell let "I dare not wait upon I would" with unfortunate results. Caution is understandable when you consider what has happened in some areas where we have risked our money. As you may have read, after spending 15 years and more than $500 million to drill 120 exploratory wells off Canada's eastern coast, oil companies are abandoning work there, at least temporarily. Drilling results offshore Nova Scotia, where Shell Canada and Shell Oil have been involved, have been terrible. As the President of Shell of Canada recently put it: "We spent $150 million out there and found nothing, so we blew the whistle." Of course, new knowledge could see us going back.

In the Gulf of Mexico, where Shell Oil pioneered the means which enabled oil men to wade out from the bayous of Louisiana into deep water, there have been outstanding successes, and Shell Oil has been perhaps the most successful. The Gulf has been one of the cradles of the technology which has made possible the harvesting of oil and gas from the sea bed in many parts of the world. In fact, in the 1960s Shell Oil ran courses to enable others to benefit from the fruits of its pioneering. (Not without proper compensation, of course!)

Outside the United States, some Shell decisions in the exploration and production field have been right, others wrong. The risks remain so great that it is not uncommon for companies which compete fiercely in the market place to share the costs of an exploration venture.

I could go on in this area of decision-making and recite a long series of successes and failures. Please understand that here is a field in which an enormous program of research and development is involved. When a venture fails to find oil, or fails to recognize its presence, it isn't for lack of a scientific effort. It's simply that what exists three miles down in the earth is still by no means a matter of scientific certainty. That fact leads one to those seemingly ridiculous decisions, where he can look very smart or very stupid. I suppose we tend to remember the latter. As one of our exploration people here in Shell Oil used to say so often, "When I'm right they never remember, when I'm wrong they never forget!"

But when one succeeds in exploration, he comes face to face with one of the areas of greatest melancholy. When one finds and develops some oil or gas, he is inclined to think that it is "his"! However, in these days there is a great tendency for the people of the country involved to consider that it is "theirs." Here is quite another area of decision-making.

What is this risk going to be over the whole spectrum of countries around the world? Will this country respect our private investment? That one not?

Remember that companies are completely at the mercy of governments, no matter how small. If the smallest country tells us to go, we have no recourse. We are concerned immediately with the safety of our staff and only later with our investment. Our only strength in such days is how much are we needed, and when our talents are needed (note I say talents; it usually is not money) we may find some way of salvaging something.

Over the past several years our lives have been a long series of such events. Our properties are taken. Many times we are able to negotiate some settlement, even to the region of a very fair one, but sometimes we get little. We may be asked to stay and help operate our former properties. Sometimes we do, as a means of having preferred access to the raw materials, or we are paid a fee.

I have dwelt on these political aspects of Shell world-wide operations because it is in this area that the multinational world differs so much from the local or domestic venture. And on my matter of decision-making, you see the problems involved. You and I who grew up in Pennsylvania or California have a certain regard for the sanctity of law and we reason that legally defensible agreements can be trusted and give us a reliable basis for planning, investment and operation. But when one goes abroad from a relatively few sophisticated lands, that assumption is no longer valid.

Now, finally, just one or two more and brief examples of decision-making.

As we have just discussed, the value today of oil production overseas to the central balance sheets is not what it was in the past. The focus has been shifted towards "downstream operations," by which I mean all the varied processes that convert crude oils into saleable products and put them on the market in 100 different countries. At this end of the business our long and large investment in research and development, in applied science, has put Shell companies in a position of unique strength. In this area, Shell is judged fairly to be outstanding.

This is not as a result of one decision but of many. Upgrading the barrel of crude oil to get the maximum proportion of premium products — gasoline, aviation turbine fuels, lubricants and specialities — out of the basic raw material, is one of the results of our long dedication to research.

Another bonus from research is the development and growth of our organic chemical business. Shell Oil here had a good start before World War II because the U.S. was somewhat unique among the scientifically strong countries in possessing raw material resources (oil and gasfields and refineries) together with an enormous market for chemical products. Our type of chemical industry thrives best in an industrial environment with major consumers of products.

The fledgling chemical business within Shell was the subject of lengthy reviews in my early years. Not infrequently some management faction would suggest that we sell it out and go back to our "proper" business, oil. However, science prevailed in the end. The largest Shell stake in chemicals is still in the United States and collectively Group chemical activities throughout the world represent the largest chemical business of any oil company, and stand very near the top in the world league of all chemical companies.

Moreover, chemicals have contributed to our usefulness to society as a multinational enterprise. One aspect I would mention is the evolution of a wide range of agrochemicals which are vital tools for the farmer in the battle against hunger in many developing countries where the world population explosion is most devasting in its effects. Shell companies together rank third in the world as manufacturers and suppliers of crop protection chemicals; our products are marketed in more than a hundred countries. The development of these products involves costly research, and long in-the-field testing before they can be put on the market. To take one example, a Shell herbicide designed to control wild oats in wheat crops was synthesized in the 1960s, introduced in 1972 after six years of research and development, and is now sold in 28 countries.

In some parts of the business, factors outside one's control can make a nonsense of scientific decision-making, no matter how skilled the planners. One recent instance has been in the inability of all large oil groups, including Shell, to balance the reduced demand for oil since 1974 against the number of tankers available to carry it.

Early in the 1970s our Group's international marine company was looking, as it regularly does, at future tanker requirements, in that case for the late '70s, with a view to placing orders then for new ships. Armed with estimates about future levels of oil requirements, management foresaw a major demand for very large crude carriers of 300,000 tons and upwards, particularly with the Suez Canal still closed and tankers bringing oil from the Middle East to Europe having to make the long haul around Southern Africa.

Since demand for oil has been increasing steadily over the last 50 years, who could dare assume that the trend would not continue? Who could have foreseen that events would turn the energy picture upside down and that much less oil than had been anticipated would be needed?

As far as Shell companies were concerned, it was estimated in 1971 that sales of oil outside North America would be about 7 million barrels per day in 1975. In the event, actual sales were around 4 million barrels per day both in 1975 and 1976. We were not alone in this, but we had in fact over-estimated our forward tanker requirements by nearly 100 per cent. In consequence, new ships have been coming off the slipways and going straight into mothballs or used for oil storage; and those at sea slow-steaming to save fuel, and other vessels prematurely scrapped to try to bring the equation into balance. Our people had simply misguessed the future. Can you fault them? I can't!

But all of these things are in the past and on the record.

As I said in connection with our Shell history in exploring for oil, one is particularly aware of failures and tends to dwell on them. Likewise, in this chapter I have concentrated on cases where we have made mistakes, for whatever reason. Of course, to bring the whole picture into better balance I should remind you that we get a lot of things right, too! Otherwise, our companies and our industry would not be the stories of success that they are. It's only the practice of the scientist to look at what remains imperfect or the areas that he understands less well. If I were trying to sell you something, rather than being a dismal scientist, from the same ingredients would have come a somewhat different and much more glamorous picture!

In summary I have wanted to make perhaps two observations about decision-making in business.

First, I have wanted to applaud and encourage in every way the use of ever more sophisticated analytical methods in reaching the impersonal decisions that are involved in the day-to-day business of all of us. These methods are good and involve disciplines that will certainly one day be in commonplace use by all efficient companies everywhere.

Second, I have tried to illustrate that there are variables in the equations for decision-making, such as political ones, where I almost totally despair of our ability to do a very good job in their evaluation. Try we must, and perhaps we can be more careful and thoughtful in this area, but it seems to be hard to expect much more than dice-throwing odds. Unfortunately, in many of our businesses that involve large exposures to certain political environments, the penalty of a poor guess can be catastrophic.

You see that this scientist has found much of that world to be lonesome, to be one where his numbers and equations aren't enough.

In the next chapter, we will examine another facet of corporate life, not decision-making, but another one where fact again doesn't always prevail. I have labelled it "Myths".

The Multinational Corporation
Its Manners, Methods
and Myths

III. Myths

III MYTHS

In the preceding chapters, I have talked first about some of the characteristics of a large multinational corporation, and then about how it makes some of the major decisions that fashion its nature and its ultimate success or failure.

I have tried to portray multinationals as they appear to the scientist; that is, the cases where facts and figures are an adequate basis for procedure, and then some cases where available facts and figures are not adequate for the best decision. But in all areas we discussed, the available facts and estimates have been used with fidelity. There is no distortion of what is known, and errors come from lack of information, or from errors or problems of prediction.

In this chapter, entitled "Myths," I want to discuss some other areas of life in the multinational corporation. I want to talk about some matters where the facts are known and are available, but where the judging mind somehow doesn't use them. In some cases it is due to ignorance, in others to carelessness, and in some cases it would seem due to intellectual dishonesty. There arise, thereby, a number of "Myths" about our companies. Let me illustrate with a variety of examples.

Myth Number One: *Large multinational corporations, with their huge financial and physical resources, control the governments of many countries in which they operate.*

This popular concept sees us as omnipotent, omnipresent, as a giant with supra-national (if not supernatural!) powers. Believe me, there are times when one wishes he had a bit of all that!

One truth is very unglamorous, very pedestrian. The largest corporation is no match for the smallest nation-state because the multinational's local affiliates are all subject to the specific local national law. Size in the business world is no criterion of power in political terms.

Years ago we used to talk about how much oil we "owned." The number today is a small fraction of what we thought it then was. We can no longer talk about "owning" oil in Rumania, most of the Middle East, in Venezuela, or even right next door in Mexico. Once we did! We still say we "own" refineries in many countries, but no longer in Indonesia, or Cuba, or Venezuela, or Brazil, or Rumania, or Mexico, or India. I wish I could tell you that we left all these places with fair remuneration for the properties taken from us, or even for the capital investments we left behind, if you contend that the oil and gas we found were not ours in the first place.

Of course, as you so well know, we have received anything but fair compensation in many cases. What we do get is heavily related to one thing: how much are we going to be needed by them in the future? Maybe they will still want us to buy oil from them, but that isn't the good reason it once was. No, their need for us will almost certainly be for our knowledge, our expertise, for the abilities that we take away with us. Indeed, knowledge is the one and only indestructible citadel!

Thus, as we are forced to leave, or alter our position in some way, we respond in a variety of ways. But the point I am making here is only that our ability to resist the will, whatever it is, of the sovereign government, however small or poor, is essentially nothing.

But our problems with governments are not only with those who confiscate our properties or send us away in some fashion. We are constantly suspected in quite different ways. There is the fear of governments that significant sectors of their economies may be subject to decisions made elsewhere or that they may be influenced by transactions — for example, through the manipulation of transfer prices or service charges — which they feel they can neither know nor control.

This ghost haunts some corridors of government power. It is the fear expressed by Tony Benn, the present U.K. Energy Minister, years ago when he said:

If we (i.e. the U.K.) had a £100 million surplus every year, if the Bank of England were overflowing with gold, we would still find our future decided by what was happening in Detroit or Tokyo, because the inter-meshing of industrial activity is getting tighter and tighter. This is the problem of the mammoth company and you cannot solve that problem alone by nationalization. If you have an international company and you nationalize the British component of it, you still have not got control over the destiny of that company.

There is no doubt, too, that centralization of financial control, and the vertical integration which characterizes some international groups, are matters for understandable government concern as to whether or not a conflict between private decision and national welfare is simply a possibility or an actuality. The central fact that we have to bear in mind, however, is that by and large no major investment can be made in any country without some regulatory consent. The only "power" the investor possesses is to refrain from invest-ing in a particular country, knowing that if he does not someone else may. Once the investment has been made — in oilfields, a refinery, a chemical plant, pipelines or service stations — these are assets on the ground which cannot be dismantled and removed, and to that extent the company has given hostages to the good faith of the host government.

Having said that, I should point out one instance in which "power" was forced upon oil companies by the inertia of governments in failing to make vital decisions affecting their energy supplies. After the Arab-Israeli war in October 1973, the failure of oil importing governments to take any role of responsibility at that time of real shortage (caused by embar-goes and production cuts by certain oil exporting countries) left the companies not only with the physical task of supply, but also with the decision as to the principles on which allocation among countries should be made. Our "power" on that occasion derived from outside, from the vacuum left by importing governments.

It is an episode which illustrated not the power of the companies to hold the world to ransom and profit from it, but their restraint in not using it to their own benefit. Our achievement in providing equality of treatment to countries (some of which demanded inequity in their own favor) was one instance where we did receive general approval.

Myth Number Two: *Large companies (multinationals and others as well) fix prices by collusion, and competition does not prevail is most parts of their operations.*

This hoary old myth still rears its head from time to time, despite all the evidence to the contrary. I can at least be fairly specific so far as the oil business is concerned.

The cost of a barrel of crude oil at origin today is roughly $13. Of that, the host country takes on average more than 90% — about $12 of the $13 — the companies on average make — as profit — 25 cents, 2 per cent of the total. Of the final price to the consumer of a representative barrel of refined oil products, let us say in the European market, which is about $27, the government of the producing country takes around $12, as I said above, and the European government takes about $10.50 in domestic taxes. The total government take is therefore nearly 85% of the customer's bill. The companies' profit is on average some 50 cents, less than 2% of the total, and the rest is cost. The ultimate price at which products are sold to the customer is thus set in principle by factors completely outside the control of the company.

In the case of gasoline, a commodity which has sparked off the most virulent price wars in the United States, the price at which the fuel is sold is fixed by competition between individual service stations, most of them independently owned. The variations in price that occur are not the results of collusion but of the free operation of competitive forces at the retail point. The rules are exactly the same as if one were selling candy or chewing gum.

I do not need to remind you that there are stringent anti-trust laws in the United States, breaches of which can lead to prison sentence. No top executive committed to private enterprise questions the goals of such laws, and the prospect of a prison sentence certainly doesn't detract from their observance.

There is also controversy about the prices at which goods move across boundaries between affiliates of multinational groups. As far as Shell companies are concerned, in order to be commercially and fiscally justifiable, the prices are based on arm's length negotiations and agreements. While Shell companies in consuming countries outside North America buy the bulk of their needs from our central oil trading company, they pay only a price that is justifiable to governments in relation to the prices available on the open market. Indeed, our local companies do buy lots from time to time on the open market to cope with swings in demand.

Governments in consumer countries concerned with balances of payments and tax matters rightly keep the closest watch on such purchases and the figures involved.

Myth Number Three: *Good citizenship acts by large companies are solely for selfish reasons and signify no public or moral conscience.*

Here is a good one, because the myth is nearer the fact! Now, before you say "I knew it all the time!", I want to be very careful in telling you what I mean.

One should preface this discussion by pointing out the elementary fact that companies such as we are considering are financial ventures, pure and simple. They are operations involving the money of the owners, and the purpose of the venture is to cause that investment of money to prosper. While the paths to financial prosperity may vary, the purpose of the exercise remains the same.

Our companies were not established to be agencies for social service. There are many such organizations and they are recognized for what they are. If we want to contribute to such purposes, and as private individuals you and I do, we look to charitable organizations or channels of one or more kinds.

It is unfortunate that some people confuse these two different types of ventures, and somehow look to my kind of company to be some sort of mixture of the two. I completely reject this philosophy, not because of any dislike of the charitable organization or any lack of interest in social betterment, but because trying to mix the two would lead one into a no-man's land where I simply wouldn't know how to operate.

If any company tells you that it cleans up its service stations, or its refinery effluents, or advertises some unusual customer service just because of public conscience — don't believe it! You all know why we, and you, do such things. These, and a thousand acts, are either required, as is payment of taxes, or are good business and require no further justification — certainly no mention of public conscience. And in many areas of our activities, I will argue against going much beyond the bounds of "good business".

Unless we were obviously hurting someone, I am not enthusiastic about decreasing further the emissions from our refineries just because they are there. You don't put scrubbers in your fire place chimneys at home because some smoke is being discharged. But we must, and do, supply all information relating to such matters; we submit our views and ideas to the society bodies concerned, and then completely abide by the decisions of the societies.

All right, you say, that is good, but it isn't enough.

What do you want us to do?

Suppose that your back yard has the odd can or barrel or lawn mower lying about. Do you build a nice fence around it so that no passer-by could possibly be offended? No, and sometimes we don't either. On balance, however, I would think that our companies are more responsible about such things than the vast majority of individuals.

If you are our shareholders, and all of us are likely in some manner to be the shareholder of each other, you will have rather conservative views of how you want us to spend your money on other than the required and the obvious acts of good citizenship.

However, there are yet other areas where public conscience, or lack of it, can be judged.

Some years ago, Shell Oil Company sponsored a nine-year-long series of programs known as "Shell's Wonderful World of Golf". I know that it brought pleasure to millions of people. Was that solely to display good citizenship? Of course not.

Nearly 25 years ago the Shell Oil Company established the Shell Companies Foundation. In the ensuing 24 years, that Foundation has given over $42 million to philanthropic ends. It has been rather heavily oriented to aid to education. Last year, that Foundation contributed over $3,300,000 to a variety of civic and educational programs.

Is the Shell Foundation solely to display good citizenship? No, not entirely, but more nearly so.

So far I have been talking about acts of good citizenship in sophisticated societies. In less developed countries the contribution made by a multinational company may be basic to the expansion of the whole economy.

To give you an example. When a Shell-operated company went into Nigeria in 1937 to look for oil, a prime area for exploration was the swamps of the Niger delta, which resembles the bayou country of Louisiana. But while Louisiana had already been tamed by man; in Nigeria the whole operation had to start from scratch. There were no detailed maps of the terrain, so aerial surveys had to be made before geological prospecting could even begin. Roads had to be cut through tropical forest to reach the drilling sites, and bridges built across a network of waterways and creeks. As a result, villagers who had had to make long journeys by canoe to do their trading could now get about on the dry land communications created by the oilmen.

Houses had to be built and medical facilities provided to combat the tropical diseases rife in an area traditionally regarded as "a white man's grave." It took 20 years before oil was found in commercial quantities. Even then the job of shipping it away was handicapped by a sandbar at the mouth of the principal river. The company dredged the entrance so that tankers could leave fully loaded, incidentally making it possible for bigger ships to reach the main port 40 miles up river.

In the process of developing an oil province, new work horizons were opened up for a people who had hitherto largely depended on subsistance farming. A trade school was established to teach artisans basic industry skills; those who showed aptitude were sent abroad for more advanced training. Nigerians became part and parcel of a new industry, which gave an additional spin-off in employment to contractors geared to supply a multitude of ancillary services.

Thus, a multinational enterprise, in pursuit of its own business objectives, helped a people to raise themselves by their own efforts to a plateau of greater prosperity.

In summary, I am suggesting that one should judge an individual or a corporation in the context of good citizenship not by the things that he must do, and consequently does, but rather how and where he goes beyond this boundary of minimum requirement into the areas where his actions are more and more motivated by clearly good morality and the urge to contribute basically and meaningfully to the strength and well-being of the societies in which he resides.

Shell companies, like others, thus contribute generously to education, to civic groups of all kinds, health centers and the arts, and so on. I am pleased to say that we do go beyond the boundary of necessity, and in a thousand ways contribute to the basic well-being of the societies in which we live.

However, it is unfair to look to the corporation for those acts that should be left to the individual. I am a Protestant, you may not be. I am a Republican, you may not be. I may have an inordinate wish to support some particular university or faculty. My corporation should not be expected or, indeed, allowed to follow my particular wishes. Thus, while our shareholders and management and employees and customers may like to see us being the good citizen that we try to be, there is a line beyond which they will rapidly cease to admire our corporate philanthropy.

Myth Number Four: *Profits of oil companies are exhorbitant, representing something like 16 cents on a gallon of gasoline here in the United States.*

I mention this example briefly only to call your attention to how misinformed the public can be. That number of 16 cents per gallon came from a public opinion poll last year here in the U.S. Those canvassed thought that a fair profit would be 11 cents. In fact, the oil companies' actual profit is more like 2 cents. Another poll estimated oil companies' average profit per dollar of total sales at 43 cents. In the case of Shell Oil Company the actual figure in 1976 was 8 cents. Many of you could cite similar examples in your own business.

Of course, "profit" is an emotive word that means different things to different people and on which no consensus exists. "Profits" to us in business mean what is left after normal business charges including depreciation, amortization of facilities, the cost of research etc., and then taxes. Perhaps some people look to an assumed oil trading profit in isolation.

In a similar vein, it seems to help little to explain that our ratio of earnings to investment is right in the middle of all industry. The earnings are large only because of the enormous investment. Incidentally, in this public opinion poll of last year, those canvassed were told that the oil companies stated — as is the case — that their profit was 2 cents per gallon. Did they believe the oil companies? Seventy-three percent said no! How can you win?

* * *

In citing some examples of the myths that surround a business such as ours, I am not implying that we have a corner on such matters, nor that we are unduly sensitive about living with such misunderstandings. As I have attempted to say, many of them are honest mistakes, or are due to an understandable lack of information.

It is somewhat more difficult, however, to excuse the person who should know better! In those cases, one always wonders about the motivation.

There is, for example, the intellectual — the professor! He is able, he speaks and writes well. He is persuasive and his arguments win considerable credence.

He can argue, and some do, that a large corporation can insulate itself from the forces of the market-place. It can control the prices of its raw materials (because of its supposed powers over the suppliers), and then manipulate the consumer to accept what it cares to produce at a price it dictates.

Why is such nonsense written and spoken? The truth is, of course, so much different!

There is a great deal of careless writing also about risk-taking and investment, the bulk of it by people who have never made a major investment-decision in their lives. It is misleading, of course, to talk about investment in general terms as if it were somehow homogeneous. It is not. Some industrial investments — pollution control and safety at work — are mandatory and do not permit of profit or pay-out analysis. But the bulk of investment is incurred either to meet a new or increased demand or to satisfy an existing demand more efficiently, or a combination of both. It is usually implemented, in terms of plant or equipment, when forward estimates show the probability of a satisfactory return, or of a better return on capital than an alternative use of the resources.

However, as we discussed in the last chapter, it seems to be impossible to assess future profitability in any exact manner. All investments involve at the end of the day an act of judgment or an act of faith. Nobody can foretell the future with sufficient accuracy to remove the uncertainty inherent in its unfolding.

Here is another example of a professional "contribution" that irks me: "The major aim of the corporate planner," wrote one of these intellectuals, "is the elimination of uncertainty." What a great contribution that statement is! We already know what the aim is, but those of us who have managed large corporations have not yet been able to identify anyone with this talent. A talent for eliminating uncertainty would be more remunerative than owning a license to print money. Corporate planners know well that the elimination of uncertainty is not of this world. The summary contribution of this particular professor was to the effect that our corporate planners approach their task by determining first the profit they wish to earn, secondly what they are going to produce and thirdly, how to foist their products on the consumer. This is so juvenile and such utter nonsense that one hardly knows how to respond.

Why so-called "scholars" take leave of objective analysis in favor of prejudice or ignorance is a phenomenon worthy of study in its own right, but we will not undertake that study here.

* * *

In total, though, should the myths and the understandings cause us great worry? I think not. Reason will not necessarily explode the myths about multinationals, nor about many other things. We are the victims of seductive oversimplifications which vanish as soon as you examine them closely, and yet they remain obstinately there.

Nevertheless, I do not think that the multinationals need to apologize for themselves. Of course they are human and fallible as we all are. But, far from being the wicked monoliths they are often made out to be, they have been a power for good in the world and created more prosperity for more people than would otherwise have been possible.

Some years ago, there was a *Newsweek* article relating to the problems that the American encounters when he goes abroad. Said *Newsweek* to such of our countrymen, "It is unworthy, and useless besides, to struggle against the greatness that is painfully being thrust upon us. The use of power provokes criticism. The world is full of people who dislike America. They will find something wrong with whatever we do."

And so it is, in some measure, with an organization like mine. We must be careful not to be too concerned with such criticism. Our primary purpose is not to be loved. It is a nice endearing thought, but we aren't engaged in a popularity contest. Sometimes we have to choose between love and respect. There is no choice; our aim must be to be respected. Love cannot be bought, but respect can be earned, by good conduct and greater understanding.

Nor, finally, should we dream of a day when our critics, and detractors, will go away and leave us quietly alone. It isn't going to happen.

Anywhere, at anytime, there are things that trouble you and me. I may rail against permissiveness, or misbehavior of the young, or Democrats — you have you own particular list — but most of the causes of your discomfort or mine come and go from one age to another.

I recall reading one time about the young man who finished school and wanted to get a job as a writer. He went to a city considered the world center of publishing and art, and of the commerce that supports both. He got there and found that the atmosphere of the city was certainly not what he had thought it would be. It was not all flashing intellect and iridescent conversation. People seemed to be snarling and snapping and telling each other that things were in a mess. There were civil problems galore. Juvenile delinquency had flared into an open scandal. People were drinking too much. Tobacco was being called a public menace. Traffic was in a frightful muddle, and if something were not done soon the city would be paralyzed. The city? London, in the year 1587. The young man's name? William Shakespeare.

As they say back in Brooklyn: "So what's new?"

Or consider this:

Our youth now love luxury. They have bad manners, contempt for authority . . . disrespect for older people . . . children nowadays are tyrants . . . they no longer arise when their elders enter the room . . . they contradict their parents, chatter before company, gobble their food, and tyrannize their teacher.

Now, I suppose that sounds like a complaint from a Cub Scout Den Mother, but it isn't; believe it or not — those were the words of Socrates in the fifth century before Christ.

Recently I read some comments made by a learned gentleman concerning what he considered conduct unbecoming to students at a great university. He deplored the lack of discipline, and especially the rioting and profanity. Does that remind you of anything you have heard about recently? You will be interested to know that the article was about students at Cambridge University, and it was published in 1682.

So what's new?

No people and no time have a monopoly on trouble.

Read the letters that George Washington wrote from Valley Forge in the winter of '77, or read "The Federalist Papers" published ten years later, and see what struggles and uncertainty and pain attended the founding of this fortunate nation.

Or read Burke and Carlyle on the French Revolution and recall the darkness, filth and tragedy beneath what we refer to now as the Age of Enlightenment in Europe.

Go back yet another hundred years, to the middle of the seventeenth century. The Elizabethan Age had shone with a brilliance that carried around the world and still outshines much of the best that man has done since. Giants walked the earth — Dryden, Locke, Milton. But in the midst of it England was torn to bits by a civil war that lasted eighteen years.

Perhaps only a few of you saw Hitler. I did. I saw a nation subverted, demolished, a nation at one moment monopolizing the world scene in medicine and science and technology, and only a decade later grovelling in shambles and in shame.

The decades just past have seen, beyond a shadow of a doubt, the greatest strides in man's history in understanding and controlling the physical world in which we live. Yet the pages are bloody with Hitlers and Stalins and, on a smaller scale, Amins and their ilk.

As with Shakespeare's time, or Socrates', or Washington's,

so with ours. Wars, violence, cruelty — being part of the human predicament — remain. And so our age like all others is, in the words of Charles Dickens, the best of times and the worst of times.

There is one class of annoyance, however, that is somewhat new and is one that isn't going to go away. That is the matter of government, and society in general, being ever more concerned with what you and I do and how we conduct our affairs. The world is finite, but it must fit in an ever increasing number of people. With communication of every sort becoming ever faster and wider, each of us is ever more aware of the neighbor right next to us; what he does is of ever greater concern to us.

So it is with the companies we keep. We will be subject to ever greater examination, interference, and control. It will involve ever more work, and it will tend to be unpleasant. However, it isn't going to go away and we must recognize and face that fact.

One final thought.

Time and again one has answered his critics, or questioners, in as honest and factual a way as the scientist in one demands. At the end of such an exchange, so often the other person says "Now I see your side of it. That's a good story you have. Why don't you tell it?"

What does one say?

I think we will all agree that the prime job of an industrialist is to run his business rather than talk about it. Some of the most successful industrialists never made a speech in their lives. Others do speak, and all of us and our organizations do, in a thousand different ways, try constantly to tell the good story that free enterprise has to tell.

I have no answer to the dilemma. The only suggestion is, of course, the obvious one. Keep on trying! A colleague of mine once described corporate public relations as "first performing honorably and morally, and then telling the world about it." You will note what part comes first.